EMMANUEL JOSEPH

Bridges of Diplomacy: Threads of Global Unity

Copyright © 2025 by Emmanuel Joseph

All rights reserved. No part of this publication may be reproduced, stored or transmitted in any form or by any means, electronic, mechanical, photocopying, recording, scanning, or otherwise without written permission from the publisher. It is illegal to copy this book, post it to a website, or distribute it by any other means without permission.

First edition

This book was professionally typeset on Reedsy.
Find out more at reedsy.com

# Contents

1. Chapter 1: The Foundation of Dialogue — 1
2. Chapter 2: Historical Milestones — 3
3. Chapter 3: The Role of Mediators — 5
4. Chapter 4: Cultural Diplomacy — 7
5. Chapter 5: Economic Diplomacy — 9
6. Chapter 6: Environmental Diplomacy — 11
7. Chapter 7: Health Diplomacy — 13
8. Chapter 8: Cyber Diplomacy — 15
9. Chapter 9: Human Rights Diplomacy — 17
10. Chapter 10: Conflict Resolution — 19
11. Chapter 11: Multilateral Diplomacy — 21
12. Chapter 12: The Future of Diplomacy — 23

# 1

# Chapter 1: The Foundation of Dialogue

Diplomacy begins with the simple act of dialogue. It is through communication that nations can voice their concerns, share their aspirations, and seek common ground. Dialogue serves as the bedrock of diplomacy, fostering mutual understanding and respect.

Active listening is a crucial element of effective dialogue. When diplomats genuinely listen to one another, they can better understand the motivations and perspectives of other nations. This empathetic approach paves the way for meaningful negotiations and collaboration.

Trust is another fundamental aspect of dialogue. Building trust between nations requires transparency, consistency, and a commitment to honoring agreements. Trustworthy dialogue can transform adversaries into allies and create a more stable international environment.

The power of dialogue is evident in its ability to prevent conflicts. By addressing grievances and misunderstandings through conversation, diplomats can resolve disputes before they escalate into violence. Dialogue acts as a preventive measure, safeguarding peace.

Dialogue also plays a role in postconflict resolution. After hostilities have ceased, dialogue helps to rebuild relationships and address the root causes of conflict. Through open communication, former enemies can work towards reconciliation and lasting peace.

Ultimately, dialogue is the lifeline of diplomacy. It is through words that bridges are built, and through understanding that unity is achieved. The foundation of dialogue is essential for weaving the threads of global unity.

# 2

# Chapter 2: Historical Milestones

Throughout history, diplomacy has shaped the course of nations and the world. One of the earliest examples is the Peace of Westphalia in 1648, which ended the Thirty Years' War and laid the foundation for modern state sovereignty and international law.

The Congress of Vienna in 1815 is another significant milestone. Following the Napoleonic Wars, European powers convened to restore stability and balance of power. The congress's outcomes influenced diplomatic practices and international relations for decades.

The Treaty of Versailles in 1919 marked the end of World War I. Although controversial, it exemplified the complexities of postwar diplomacy. The treaty aimed to prevent future conflicts but also highlighted the challenges of achieving lasting peace.

In 1945, the establishment of the United Nations signaled a new era of multilateral diplomacy. The UN provided a platform for nations to collaborate on global issues, from peacekeeping to human rights. Its creation underscored the importance of collective action.

The Camp David Accords of 1978 demonstrated the potential of diplomacy to resolve deeply entrenched conflicts. The accords, brokered by the United States, led to a peace treaty between Egypt and Israel, showcasing the transformative power of diplomatic efforts.

These historical milestones illustrate how diplomacy has evolved and adapted to changing global dynamics. They remind us that through persistent and dedicated efforts, diplomatic bridges can be built even in the most challenging times.

# 3

# Chapter 3: The Role of Mediators

Mediators play a crucial role in the diplomatic landscape. Acting as neutral third parties, they facilitate negotiations between conflicting nations, helping them find mutually acceptable solutions. Mediators bring a sense of impartiality and expertise to the table.

The success of mediation depends on the mediator's ability to build trust. By demonstrating neutrality and fairness, mediators can gain the confidence of all parties involved. Trust is essential for creating an environment conducive to productive negotiations.

Mediators employ various techniques to foster cooperation. They may use shuttle diplomacy, where they move between parties to convey messages and proposals. This method allows for continuous dialogue without direct confrontation, easing tensions.

Another effective approach is interestbased negotiation. Mediators focus on identifying the underlying interests of each party rather than their stated positions. This strategy helps to uncover common ground and develop creative solutions that satisfy all parties.

Mediators also play a key role in conflict resolution. They assist in drafting peace agreements and ensuring that the terms are acceptable and implementable. Their involvement often extends beyond negotiations, helping to monitor and support the implementation of agreements.

The impact of mediators is profound. By guiding conflicting parties through the complexities of negotiation, they pave the way for peaceful resolutions and longterm stability. Mediators exemplify the transformative power of diplomacy in action.

# 4

# Chapter 4: Cultural Diplomacy

Cultural diplomacy is the exchange of ideas, values, and traditions between nations. It enhances mutual understanding and fosters connections that transcend political and economic interests. Cultural diplomacy celebrates the richness of diverse heritages and promotes global unity.

Art and culture are powerful tools of diplomacy. Cultural exchange programs, art exhibitions, and performances allow nations to share their unique perspectives and foster appreciation for each other's traditions. These exchanges build bridges of friendship and respect.

Education is another key component of cultural diplomacy. Student exchange programs and academic partnerships create opportunities for crosscultural learning and collaboration. By studying and working together, individuals from different backgrounds can develop lifelong bonds.

Cultural diplomacy also includes language initiatives. Promoting language learning and proficiency helps to break down communication barriers and facilitate deeper understanding. Language is a gateway to culture, and fluency opens doors to meaningful interactions.

In times of strife, cultural diplomacy can be a beacon of hope. It provides a platform for dialogue and reconciliation, allowing nations to find common ground and celebrate shared humanity. Cultural diplomacy reminds us of our interconnectedness and the value of diversity.

Through cultural diplomacy, nations can build a tapestry of global unity. By embracing and promoting their cultural heritage, they contribute to a more harmonious and understanding world. Cultural diplomacy weaves the threads of unity that bind us together.

# 5

# Chapter 5: Economic Diplomacy

Economic diplomacy focuses on fostering international trade, investment, and economic cooperation. It aims to enhance economic prosperity and stability by negotiating trade agreements, resolving economic disputes, and promoting sustainable development.

Trade agreements are vital tools of economic diplomacy. They reduce barriers to trade, such as tariffs and quotas, and create a level playing field for businesses. By opening markets and encouraging competition, trade agreements stimulate economic growth and innovation.

Investment promotion is another key aspect of economic diplomacy. Attracting foreign direct investment (FDI) can bring capital, technology, and expertise to a country. Economic diplomats work to create favorable conditions for investment and build investor confidence.

Economic diplomacy also involves addressing global challenges such as poverty and inequality. By collaborating on development projects and providing financial assistance, nations can work together to uplift vulnerable populations and create more equitable societies.

Sustainable development is a cornerstone of modern economic diplomacy. Diplomats advocate for environmentally friendly policies and practices that balance economic growth with environmental protection. Promoting sustainable trade and investment is essential for longterm prosperity.

Economic diplomacy requires a deep understanding of global markets and economic policies. Successful diplomats must navigate complex negotiations and balance competing interests to achieve mutually beneficial outcomes. Their efforts contribute to a more interconnected and resilient global economy.

# 6

# Chapter 6: Environmental Diplomacy

Environmental diplomacy addresses global environmental challenges through international cooperation. It involves negotiating agreements, coordinating policies, and fostering collaboration to protect the planet and ensure a sustainable future for all.

Climate change is a central focus of environmental diplomacy. International agreements such as the Paris Agreement aim to limit global warming and reduce greenhouse gas emissions. Diplomats work to secure commitments from nations to take meaningful action on climate change.

Biodiversity conservation is another critical area of environmental diplomacy. Protecting endangered species and preserving ecosystems requires coordinated efforts across borders. Diplomatic initiatives promote conservation policies and support international cooperation on biodiversity.

Pollution control is essential for safeguarding human health and the environment. Environmental diplomacy addresses issues such as air and water pollution, encouraging nations to adopt stricter regulations and invest in cleaner technologies. Collaborative efforts are key to reducing pollution and its impacts.

Sustainable development goals (SDGs) provide a framework for environmental diplomacy. These goals, adopted by the United Nations, guide diplomatic efforts to balance economic growth, social development, and environmental protection. SDGs emphasize the importance of sustainability in all aspects of development.

Environmental diplomacy requires innovative approaches and longterm commitment. Diplomats must navigate complex scientific, economic, and political considerations to develop effective solutions. Their work is vital for addressing global environmental challenges and promoting sustainability.

Through environmental diplomacy, nations can build a more sustainable and resilient world. By working together to protect the planet, they contribute to a legacy of stewardship and responsibility for future generations. Environmental diplomacy weaves the threads of unity that connect us all.

# 7

# Chapter 7: Health Diplomacy

Health diplomacy focuses on addressing global health challenges through international cooperation. It involves negotiating agreements, coordinating responses to health crises, and promoting equitable access to healthcare and resources.

The COVID19 pandemic underscored the importance of health diplomacy. Nations collaborated on vaccine development and distribution, shared information on best practices, and provided support to overwhelmed healthcare systems. Health diplomacy was crucial in managing the global response to the pandemic.

International organizations play a key role in health diplomacy. The World Health Organization (WHO) coordinates global health efforts, provides guidance, and supports member states in addressing public health issues. Collaboration with international organizations enhances the effectiveness of health diplomacy.

Equitable access to healthcare is a central goal of health diplomacy. Addressing disparities in health services and resources requires coordinated efforts to ensure that all populations have access to essential healthcare. Health diplomats advocate for policies that promote health equity and social justice.

Health diplomacy also addresses global health threats such as infectious diseases, noncommunicable diseases, and environmental health risks. By coordinating responses and sharing resources, nations can mitigate the impacts of health crises and improve public health outcomes.

Capacity building is an essential aspect of health diplomacy. Strengthening healthcare systems and training health professionals in low and middleincome countries enhances their ability to respond to health challenges. Health diplomats support capacitybuilding initiatives to improve global health resilience.

Through health diplomacy, nations can build a healthier and more equitable world. By fostering international cooperation on health issues, they contribute to a more resilient global community. Health diplomacy weaves the threads of unity that promote wellbeing for all.

# 8

# Chapter 8: Cyber Diplomacy

Cyber diplomacy addresses the challenges and opportunities of the digital age through international cooperation. It involves negotiating agreements on cybersecurity, data protection, and internet governance to ensure a safe, open, and inclusive digital environment.

Cybersecurity is a critical aspect of cyber diplomacy. Nations must collaborate to establish norms and standards for responsible state behavior in cyberspace. This cooperation helps to mitigate cyber threats, prevent cyber warfare, and promote a secure online environment.

Data protection and privacy are also key concerns. As data becomes an increasingly valuable asset, protecting individuals' privacy and securing data from unauthorized access is paramount. Diplomatic efforts aim to create international frameworks that balance innovation with privacy protection.

Internet governance is another vital area of cyber diplomacy. Ensuring that the internet remains a free and open platform for communication, innovation, and economic growth requires collective action. Diplomatic initiatives promote policies that support a fair and inclusive digital ecosystem.

Cyber diplomacy involves multiple stakeholders, including governments, private sector companies, and civil society organizations. Effective cyber diplomacy requires collaboration among these actors to address the complex and evolving challenges of the digital age.

Through cyber diplomacy, nations can harness the potential of technology to drive progress while safeguarding against risks. By working together, they can build a secure and inclusive digital future that benefits all. Cyber diplomacy weaves the threads of unity that connect us in the digital realm.

# 9

# Chapter 9: Human Rights Diplomacy

Human rights diplomacy advocates for the protection and promotion of human rights worldwide. It involves engaging with governments, international organizations, and civil society to address human rights violations and promote social justice.

International treaties such as the Universal Declaration of Human Rights provide a framework for human rights diplomacy. Diplomats work to ensure that these principles are upheld, advocating for the rights of marginalized and vulnerable populations.

Human rights diplomacy also involves addressing systemic issues that contribute to human rights abuses. Diplomats engage in dialogue and negotiation to promote legal and institutional reforms that protect human rights and hold violators accountable.

Supporting human rights defenders is a crucial aspect of this work. These individuals and organizations often face significant risks in their efforts to promote human rights. Diplomats provide support and amplify their voices, ensuring that their work is recognized and protected.

Human rights diplomacy is not without challenges. Diplomats must navigate complex political landscapes and balance competing interests. However, their efforts are essential for creating a more just and equitable world where the dignity and rights of all individuals are respected.

Through human rights diplomacy, nations can build a global community based on shared values of equality, justice, and human dignity. By advocating for human rights, diplomats contribute to a world where everyone can live free from fear and oppression.

# 10

# Chapter 10: Conflict Resolution

Conflict resolution is at the heart of diplomacy. It involves addressing the root causes of conflicts, negotiating peace agreements, and promoting reconciliation to prevent future violence. Diplomats play a crucial role in facilitating these processes.

Peace agreements are essential tools for resolving conflicts. These agreements outline the terms of peace and provide a roadmap for rebuilding and recovery. Diplomats work tirelessly to ensure that the terms are fair, comprehensive, and implementable.

Reconciliation is a vital aspect of conflict resolution. Healing the wounds of war and building trust between former adversaries requires sustained efforts. Through dialogue and cooperation, diplomats promote reconciliation and create the conditions for lasting peace.

Conflict resolution also involves addressing underlying issues such as inequality, injustice, and resource disputes. By tackling these root causes, diplomats can prevent conflicts from recurring and create a more stable and peaceful environment.

Mediators and peacekeepers play important roles in conflict resolution. Mediators facilitate negotiations and help conflicting parties reach agreements, while peacekeepers provide security and support the implementation of peace agreements. Their combined efforts contribute to the success of diplomatic initiatives.

Through conflict resolution, diplomats pave the way for a more peaceful world. By addressing the causes of conflict and promoting reconciliation, they build bridges of understanding and cooperation. Conflict resolution weaves the threads of unity that bind us together in peace.

# 11

# Chapter 11: Multilateral Diplomacy

Multilateral diplomacy involves working with multiple countries and international organizations to address global challenges. It emphasizes collective action and cooperation to achieve common goals, leveraging the strengths of diverse actors.

The United Nations is a key platform for multilateral diplomacy. It provides a forum for nations to discuss and coordinate responses to global issues such as peace and security, sustainable development, and human rights. Multilateral diplomacy at the UN promotes collaboration and consensus building.

Regional organizations also play a significant role in multilateral diplomacy. Entities such as the European Union, African Union, and Association of Southeast Asian Nations facilitate cooperation among member states, addressing regional challenges and promoting integration.

Multilateral agreements are essential tools of multilateral diplomacy. These agreements, such as the Paris Agreement on climate change, bring together multiple countries to commit to collective action. They provide a framework for coordinated efforts and shared responsibilities.

Multilateral diplomacy involves navigating complex negotiations and balancing diverse interests. Diplomats must work to build consensus and find common ground, ensuring that the outcomes are fair and equitable. Successful multilateral diplomacy requires patience, skill, and a deep understanding of global dynamics.

The strength of multilateral diplomacy lies in its ability to address global challenges that no single nation can solve alone. By working together, nations can create comprehensive solutions that benefit everyone. Multilateral diplomacy weaves the threads of unity that connect us in our shared pursuit of a better world.

# 12

# Chapter 12: The Future of Diplomacy

The future of diplomacy will be shaped by emerging challenges and opportunities. Issues such as climate change, technological advancements, and geopolitical shifts will require innovative approaches and renewed commitment to international cooperation.

Adapting to these changes will be essential. Diplomats must embrace new tools and strategies, leveraging technology and data to enhance their efforts. Continued investment in diplomatic training and capacitybuilding will ensure that diplomats are equipped to navigate the complexities of the modern world.

The role of nonstate actors will also become increasingly important. Nongovernmental organizations, multinational corporations, and civil society will play a larger role in shaping international relations. Diplomats will need to engage with these actors to build inclusive and effective partnerships.

Sustainability will be a central focus of future diplomacy. Addressing global challenges such as climate change, resource scarcity, and environmental degradation will require coordinated efforts and longterm commitment. Diplomats will play a key role in promoting sustainable policies and practices.

Inclusivity and equity will also be critical. Ensuring that all voices are heard and represented in diplomatic processes will enhance the legitimacy and effectiveness of international cooperation. Diplomats must work to address disparities and promote social justice.

Ultimately, the future of diplomacy lies in our ability to build bridges of understanding and cooperation. By fostering dialogue, trust, and collaboration, we can create a more peaceful and interconnected world. The threads of global unity will continue to weave a tapestry of hope and progress for future generations.

www.ingramcontent.com/pod-product-compliance
Lightning Source LLC
LaVergne TN
LVHW020743090526
838202LV00057BA/6198